BE A SUCCESSFUL SUPERVISOR

Better Management Skills

This highly popular range of inexpensive paperbacks covers all areas of basic management. Practical, easy to read and instantly accessible, these guides will help managers to improve their business or communication skills. Those marked * are available on audio cassette.

The books in this series can be tailored to specific company requirements. For further details, please contact the publisher, Kogan Page, telephone 0171 278 0433, fax 0171 837 6348.

Be a Successful Supervisor
Be Positive
Building High Performance Teams
Business Creativity
Business Etiquette
Coaching Your Employees
Conducting Effective Interviews
Counselling Your Staff
Creative Decision-making
Creative Thinking in Business
Delegating for Results
Develop Your Assertiveness
Effective Employee Participation
Effective Meeting Skills
Effective Performance Appraisals*
Effective Presentation Skills
Empowerment
First Time Supervisor
Get Organised!
Goals and Goal Setting
How to Communicate Effectively*
How to Develop a Positive Attitude*
How to Develop Assertiveness
How to Manage Organisational Change
How to Motivate People*
How to Plan Your Competitive Strategy
How to Understand Financial Statements
How to Write a Staff Manual
Improving Employee Performance
Improving Relations at Work
Leadership Skills for Women
Make Every Minute Count*
Making TQM Work
Managing Cultural Diversity at Work
Managing Disagreement Constructively
Managing Organisational Change
Managing Part-time Employees
Managing Quality Customer Service
Marketing for Success
Memory Skills in Business
Mentoring
Office Management
Personnel Testing
Process Improvement
Productive Planning
Project Management
Quality Customer Service
Rate Your Skills as a Manager
Sales Training Basics
Self-managing Teams
Successful Negotiation
Successful Presentation Skills
Successful Telephone Techniques
Systematic Problem-solving and Decision-making
Team Building
Training Methods that Work
The Woman Manager

BE A SUCCESSFUL SUPERVISOR

Peter Cusins

KOGAN PAGE

First published in 1994
Reprinted 1995, 1996

Kogan Page Limited
120 Pentonville Road
London N1 9JN

British Library Cataloguing in Publication Data

A CIP record for this book is available from the British Library.

ISBN 0 7494 1492 8

Typeset by BookEns Ltd, Royston, Herts.
Printed and bound in Great Britain by Clays Ltd, St. Ives plc.

Contents

CHAPTER 1
The Supervisor's Job

This chapter addresses three questions:

- What is supervision?
- Where does the supervisor fit in?
- What does the supervisor do?

One way of thinking about work is that *work is effort put into achieving some sort of result.* When we look around us at work in our organisation, where a number of people work together, people seem to be doing two kinds of work.

On one hand, we may see a floor sweeper putting effort into achieving clean floors, an eye surgeon putting effort into achieving the restoration of someone's sight, a computer operator struggling to get the computer to print a report, or a typist putting effort into achieving a readable document. These people are achieving results through their own efforts, and not through the efforts of someone else. This kind of work is often called *operating work.*

On the other hand, we see people who mainly seem to be in discussion with others. They may be asking the sweeper to help at the desk because the receptionist is late. Or they may be discussing the possibility of getting another computer system to make the computer operator's job easier. Their function is to help the operating people to work more effectively. This work is known as *supervisory work.*

Operating work
Work done to secure results through our *own* efforts and not through the efforts of others.

Supervisory work
The effort of planning, organising, leading, co-ordinating and controlling in order to secure results *through others.*

What is supervision?

The responsibilities of the supervisor

Top management is responsible for keeping an eye on the economic and business environment, and formulating business strategies to keep the company alive and profitable. Middle management is responsible for using the business strategy to formulate the major goals, policies and procedures of the company, and to ensure that the necessary human and material resources are made available for their implementation.

The workforce is responsible for producing the products or services required by the customers and offered by the company in exchange for money.

Supervisors are responsible for providing the link between management and the workforce.

Supervisors
Understand strategic goals, policies and procedures and communicate them to the workforce.
Ensure that quality, time and budget targets are met.

Management
Keep aware of the business and its wider environment.

Formulate goals and policies.

Keep the company healthy and keep the business profitable.

Resolve strategic problems.

Workforce
Understand the objectives and operating tasks required to ensure achievement of the company's goals.

Perform their tasks safely and efficiently.

Resolve workface problems.

Resolve tactical problems.
Identify strategic problems from tactical ones, and communicate them to management.

Responsibilities in an organisation

The functions of a supervisor

Supervision means being able to *look ahead* and *plan*, *look around* to *organise* and *co-ordinate* the efforts of our people, *look back* regularly to *monitor* that we are doing what we planned to do, and, if not, to *look into* things and put them right by taking *control* and *problem-solving*.

Central to all of these, and essential for their effectiveness, is our ability to *lead*, to *communicate* and to *learn*.

Looking into

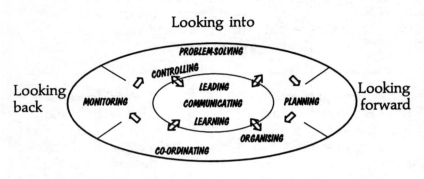

Looking back · Looking forward

Looking around

The functions of a supervisor: super-vision

The people who you supervise will be doing the work that achieves the production required from your section. Your job is to help them, and to ensure that the work gets done. The tools in this book are to help you to do this effectively.

CHAPTER 2
Start-up Induction

Description

When someone comes to work with us for the first time, induction is the start-up tool we use to ensure a good start for all of us.

Background

Inducting a new person is like turning on the power when we first arrive at work. After we unlock and come in the door, we may turn on the lights and the heating. Then we switch on the photocopier or computers so that they can warm up, and so on. Similarly, when a new employee arrives to work with us, we can press the five start-up switches necessary for a good working relationship with them. These switches relate to the five main issues of concern to most people when they start in a new job. The brighter the lights in these five areas, the more easily we can remove the initial anxiety and distraction associated with a new job situation.

The five switches
(What the new person needs to know)

1. What goes on here?
   The company's core mission. Your department's core

mission. Exactly what is produced or supplied. The goals and targets.

2. **Where do I belong?**
   Position in the department. Who they report to. Who they work with. Who reports to them. Key people they need to know about. Where their desk or workplace is. Where they can relax, eat, use the toilet, smoke.

3. **What is expected of me?**
   What their overall job is. What their key tasks and responsibilities are. Who needs to be told what and when. What their performance standards are, and what the behaviour standards are (dress, etc).

4. **What do I get in return?**
   Their salary, bonuses and perks. Any other rewards, such as prizes, etc.

5. **Where do I go for help?**
   Your phone number(s) and when and how to get hold of you. Actual names and phone numbers of other people who may be responsible to help them with particular problems like transport, welfare, illness, etc.

When to use start-up induction

- Whenever someone new arrives to work with you.
- Whenever you arrive at a new job, you can use the same process in reverse, to make sure that you get a good start-up yourself.

How to use start-up induction

Step 1. Make sure you have the information – if you don't, get it
If you were not involved in selecting the new person, this may mean consulting your own boss, or talking to personnel.

Step 2. Make sure you put aside enough time to give them your full attention
Put aside about half an hour. If you are busy or have a crisis to

attend to, arrange for another time (the next day if necessary). Trying to do the induction in a hurry is not effective and ultimately takes more time.

Step 3. Make sure you discuss each question — don't leave it to them

In a new situation, people may feel intimidated by the newness, and may be unsure about what they can or cannot ask. So talk about all five switches, even if they don't ask.

Step 4. Check that they understand

Ask open questions (that is, questions that require an answer of more than one word), or ask them to summarise what you have said. Invite their questions and answer them — or find someone who can.

Step 5. Introduce them to everyone else — that means *everyone*!

Checklist for effective use ·

- Were you able to talk privately and unhurriedly?
- Did you use their own name when speaking to the person?
- Did you invite and answer all of their questions and concerns?
- Was the information you gave them, for each question, *specific and detailed*?
- Did you discuss *all* five switch-on questions?

CHAPTER 3
Mutual Objective Setting

Description

Mutual objective setting is an interpersonal tool that provides a sound starting point for managing the performance of a team member or employee.

Background

Supervising is the art and craft of using other people's efforts to complete the tasks for which we are accountable. We seem to be more effective as supervisors if we have a clear starting-point for this process.

Mutual objective setting is a way of providing a starting-point that allows the worker and supervisor to be confident that their efforts will achieve the desired results and not be wasted. It gives clear direction to the employee's efforts, and provides a reference point for the assessment of their performance.

When to use mutual objective setting

- Whenever a new employee starts a job.
- Whenever someone new joins your department.
- Whenever you take over the management of another department or section.

- Whenever a new task is to be allocated to someone.
- At times of job reviews.
- At least once a year for all your staff.

How to use mutual objective setting

Mutual objective setting is conducted in five straightforward steps:

Step 1. Ensure clarity on the overall goals of your department or section
Start by asking the employee to describe to you the overall goals of your section. If they are unable to do so, or if they are inaccurate, restate the goals carefully. Use diagrams or figures if they would be helpful. Then ask the employee to restate what you have told them in their own words.

Only proceed to the next step once it is clear to you that they fully understand the section's goals.

Step 2. Make task lists independently
Ask the employee to write a list of the tasks they could do in order to help achieve the sectional goals. While they are busy, make your own list of what you think their key tasks should be.

During this time, each of you should work separately and not interrupt the other's flow of thought. The first to finish should wait quietly until the other has completed their list.

Step 3. Discuss and agree on a mutually acceptable list
Listen to the employee's list first, then tell them what is on your list. Ask for their comments on your list, and listen to them. Then make comments on their list if necessary. Do not start commenting on the lists until *both* lists have been heard.

Discuss the lists, and agree on a final list of the employee's key tasks. If you are unable to come to an amicable agreement, avoid imposing your own ideas. Accept that a difference exists, end the meeting, and discuss the problem with your manager.

Step 4. Clarify the objective of each task. Restate it in words that describe

(a) *Action*. This is what the person will *do* while carrying out the task.

(b) *Result*. This is what the job will be like after the task is done.

(c) *Standards*. These are what you will check or measure to ensure that the job has been done properly.

During steps 1 to 3 it is not really important how the tasks are stated, as long as you understand each other. At step 4, however, it is necessary to be precise for two reasons.

● It is the starting-point for the task – it tells the employee exactly what has to be done, even if you are not available.
● It is also the referent for monitoring the task, so that you both can see how the task is progressing and when it has been completed satisfactorily.

An easy way to test whether the objective has been clearly stated is to ask yourself, 'When this task has been completed, will both the supervisor and employee be able to know that it has been completed satisfactorily, even if the other is not present?'

Step 5. Ensure understanding and agreement
Once each objective has been restated and written down in terms of *Action–Result–Standard*, you may ask for any final comments from the employee before making a copy for each of you.

Checklist for effective use

● Did you allow enough time (20–30 minutes) for the activity?
● Did you know what the 'official' overall goals of your department were?
● Did you allow your employee to remain uninterrupted while working on their list?

- Did you make a list of the tasks you want them to do?
- Did you *listen* to their suggestions about how they could help achieve departmental goals?
- Did you put the objective(s) for each task in writing?
- Did you ensure that each objective clearly describes the three basic elements of *action*, *result* and *standard* required?
- Did you ensure that the employee understands the objective(s), by asking them to explain it to you in their own words?

Summary

1. Clarify your departmental goals.
2. Make task lists independently.
3. Agree a mutually acceptable list.
4. Clarify each task in terms of Action–Result–Standards.
5. Ensure understanding.

By working faithfully eight hours a day, you may eventually get to be a boss ... and work 12 hours a day.

CHAPTER 4
Project Planning

Description

A project plan is a blueprint for our efforts. In it we make clear what our efforts are intended to achieve (the project), and how we propose to complete the project within the specified limits of quality, cost and time (the plan).

Background

A project is an undertaking that has a beginning and an end, and is carried out within specific quality, cost and time constraints. In formulating the project plan, we look forward and envisage how we can *best* use our resources to complete the project.

Planning the project is the first of three stages of project management (see p. 21).

Each part of the project is specified in detail during the planning phase. These specifications then form the basis for monitoring and controlling the project as work proceeds during the implementing stage.

When to use project planning

Project planning should be used whenever you have a job to do that has a definite end-point.

Stage 1 **Planning**	Stage 2 **Implementing**	Stage 3 **Completing**
Define the objective	Allocate responsibilities	Deliver the output
Define the quality specifications	Allocate resources	Complete the administration
Plan the time dimension	Monitor performance	Evaluate the experience
Plan the cost dimension	Take corrective action	Learn from the experience

How to do project planning

Step 1. Define the objective
The purpose of defining the objective of a project is to ensure that we know what the customer wants delivered to them. The objective describes the end-point of the project — what results from our efforts. We need to make sure we know the answer to a number of questions:
   (a) Who — exactly — is the customer?
   (b) What — exactly — does the customer want?
   (c) How — exactly — will the customer know they have got what they asked for?

Step 2. Define the quality specifications
The purpose of defining the quality specifications is to ensure that the project output will perform effectively — that it will do what it is meant to do.
Note. The quality specifications are defined by the customer, not by us. We may give advice or make suggestions from our experience, but that is all. The final decision about quality specifications belongs to the customer. Again, we need to know the answers to a number of questions:

(a) What will the project output be required to do?
(b) What will be the performance standards of the project output?
(c) How will they be tested and measured?
(d) What types and quality of materials are required?

Step 3. Define the time dimension
The purpose of planning the time dimension is to determine the shortest possible time necessary to complete the project, and write this into a project schedule.

(a) Break the work down into sub-units, and decide the time required to complete each sub-unit. (These are often called *work-bundles* if large, and *tasks* if small.) If you have no experience in managing a particular project, this is when it is worthwhile seeking the advice of someone with experience.
(b) Next decide the sequence in which the sub-units must be completed. Write the project schedule as a bar chart, with horizontal bars indicating the duration of each sub-unit. (On large projects, it may help to use flow charting methods such as programme evaluation and review technique (PERT) and critical path plans, or computer-aided project sequencing. These are beyond the scope of this summary, but their skills are fairly easy to acquire.)

Step 4. Plan the cost dimension
The purpose of planning a budget carefully is to ensure two things: that you don't *overestimate* costs and lose the contract, and that you don't *underestimate* the costs and be unable to finish the project (or go bankrupt).

(a) Decide on the cost components you will need to consider for each sub-unit. The usual cost components are: labour, overheads, materials, supplies, equipment hire, administration and special costs.
(b) Use your work breakdown and project schedule to estimate the cost of each sub-unit, and then estimate the cost of the entire project.

Step 5. Prepare a planning summary worksheet

Write up a summary worksheet that includes the work sub-units (steps or components) and the time and cost budgeted to each one. This provides you with the planning information you need to go on with stages 2 and 3 of project management.

Checklist for effective use

- Does what you are planning to do have a clear end-point?
- Do you know exactly who the customer is?
- Have you had direct contact with the customer to ensure that you understand what they want?
- Have you given the customer the time and the opportunity to make their quality specifications clear to you?
- Are you clear about the type and quality of materials required?
- Do you understand clearly the intended use of the project output (building, construction, machine, diagram, report, etc)?
- Are you clear about how the project output will be measured and tested?
- Are you reasonably confident that your estimates of time are realistic?
- Are you confident that you have taken all costs into consideration for your budget?
- Have you prepared a planning summary worksheet?

A specimen planning summary worksheet is offered on page 25.

Summary

Supervision may involve:
- **Operations**
  Work undertakings that tend to recur in a cyclical fashion.
- **Projects**
  Work undertakings that have a definite beginning and end.

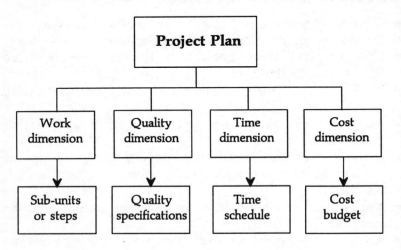

> If you do nothing, nothing will happen.
> If you do something, something will happen.
> ... but not what you intended.

Sample Planning Summary Worksheet

Project title:				

Objective:				

Quality specifications:				

Work sub-unit or step	Start date	Finish date	Budget	Responsi-bility

CHAPTER 5
Delegation

Description

Delegation is the act of transferring responsibility for the performance of a task to someone else. Supervision, on the other hand, is the skill of ensuring that the task is responsibly completed by them.

Background

Two of the major implications of being a manager are:

● Being responsible for achieving goals and targets that require more work (the performance of more tasks) than we are able to do ourselves.
● Allocating one or more other people to assist us in completing our tasks (our subordinates).

While the art of delegation is to transfer to our subordinate the responsibility of performing some of our tasks, the skill of delegation is to do it in such a way that there is good reason to believe that they will be successfully completed.

Skilled delegation, therefore, is the starting point for effective supervision.

Good delegation now → Easier supervision later

When to use delegation

Delegation is indicated for *all* operational, technical or routine tasks that have to be done, *unless* there are good reasons not to. Enjoying a particular task is the *worst* reason for not delegating it.

Good reasons for *not* delegating are:
- Your subordinate is unable to perform the task; he or she does not have the training or experience necessary for that particular task. (In this case, delegation is inappropriate; they require training first.)
- Your subordinate is able to perform the task but, for some reason (such as lack of confidence or feeling ill) is reluctant to do it. (Delegation in this situation is also inappropriate; problem-solving is needed prior to delegation.)
- The task involves working with information requiring a high level of secrecy/security to which the subordinate should not have access. (We have to do these tasks ourselves.)

How to use delegation

Step 1. Explain what is to be done — the result required and the standards expected.

Step 2. Ask the person to explain back to you, in their own words, what has been delegated to them.

Step 3. Discuss what resources (tools, transport, extra help, finance) they will need, and ensure that they know where and how to get hold of them.

Step 4. Tell them what to do if anything unforeseen or unexpected happens, and double-check that they understand.

Step 5. Once you are satisfied that they are clear about what is to be done, and know how to get help, *leave them alone to get on with it*. (If not, start again.)

Checklist for effective use

- Are you clear exactly what it is you want to delegate?
- Does the person have the training and experience necessary to do the task?
- Is the person willing to do the task?
- Has the person described the objective back to you to your satisfaction? (Are you sure they understand the actions, results and standards you require?)
- Do they know exactly where and how to get the resources they need for the task?
- Do they have the necessary authority to get any resources they may need?
- Do they know how to get hold of you (or what other action to take) if something unforeseen happens?
- Are you leaving them alone to get on with it? (Are you busy doing something else constructive while they are working?)

Summary

When to delegate

Appropriate delegation	Inappropriate delegation
• The person has the necessary ability, training and experience to do the task.	• The person does not have the ability, training and experience to do the task.
• The person is willing and confident to do the task.	• The person is either unwilling or insecure about doing the task.

How to delegate
Carry out the following steps in order:

1. Explain the result required.
2. Check understanding.
3. Discuss resources.
4. Discuss the unexpected.
5. Leave them alone.

> You cannot build character and courage by taking away a man's initiative and independence. You cannot help men permanently by doing for them what they should be doing for themselves.
>
> Abraham Lincoln

CHAPTER 6
Active Listening

Description

Listening is a combination of hearing and understanding exactly what someone is saying to us. It is the means of communication by which we ensure that we have understood not only their words, but also their *meaning*. When we have listened effectively, we will not only have heard exactly what the other person has *said*, but will also have understood exactly what they *mean*.

Background

Communication has two main areas, namely media communication (radio, TV, books, magazines, etc) and interpersonal communication (conversation between two people), each of which has its own world of study, skills, and culture. The two main sets of skills in interpersonal communication are sending skills (talking or speaking) and listening skills. The listening skills are dealt with in this chapter.

		1.1.1 TELEVISION
	1.1 MEDIA	1.1.2 NEWSPAPERS
	COMMUNICATION	1.1.3 BOOKS
1. COMMUNICATION		etc
	1.2 INTERPERSONAL	1.2.1 SENDING SKILLS
	COMMUNICATION	1.2.2 LISTENING SKILLS

In true dialogue between two people, the role of each person alternates between that of speaker and that of listener. While one speaks, the other listens; and then the roles reverse. When each of two people in a conversation merely alternate between speaking and waiting (while one speaks, the other doesn't listen but just waits) there is no real communication — just a series of monologues by each. *Listening is what transforms conversation from serial monologues (idle chatter) into true dialogue (real communication).*

	Person A	Person B
True dialogue (Real communication)	Listens Speaks Listens Speaks	Speaks Listens Speaks Listens
Serial monologues (No real communication)	Speaks Waits Speaks Waits	Waits Speaks Waits Speaks

When to use active listening

- Whenever you ask a question.
- When someone asks 'Can I have a word with you?'
- When you are conducting an enquiry of any sort.
- Whenever you really want to hear and understand what someone else has to say; that is, whenever you want to understand not only what they say, but also what they mean.

How to use active listening

By listening actively, we mean that, not only do you hear and understand the other person, you *also let them know that you are hearing and understanding them.* Active listening involves using six skills in different combinations. They are often used in the following sequence:

1. Use silence
so that you can concentrate on what the other person is saying.

2. Maintain eye contact
to convey to them that your attention is with them, and not somewhere else.

3. Give non-verbal affirmation
such as smiling, nodding, 'uh huh' and so on.

4. Use rephrasing
by repeating, in your own words what you have understood them to say. *Rephrasing* what they have said allows both of you to check that you have really understood. (Until then, you can only *assume* you have understood them.)

5. Summarise
by repeating the main points of what they have told you, to reinforce your understanding, and to convey to them that you have given them your attention.

6. Use reflection
If the person stops speaking, and the silence becomes so prolonged that you begin to feel uncomfortable, simply *repeat the last word or phrase that they said,* and wait again. Don't say anything else, just *'reflect'* the last word or phrase they used and wait expectantly. (Once people realise that we really want to hear what they have to say, it is not unusual for them to take quite a long time to think it through before speaking, especially if it concerns something personal.)

Other techniques used in this situation are:

- Say 'yes ... and?' and wait for them to continue.
- Use the opportunity to rephrase or summarise.

A note on asking questions

When you don't understand what the other person is saying, or when you want more clarity, you may stop listening in order to ask questions. If you do ask questions, always start with *open* questions. Open questions do not have a one-word answer, and usually start with *what, when, how* or *who*. Having asked the question, you then revert to active listening in order to hear and understand the answer.

Checklist for effective use

- Did you remain silent and avoid interrupting?
- Did you maintain eye contact 90 per cent of the time they were speaking?
- Did you give the occasional nod, smile or verbal encouragement to show you were still paying attention?
- Did you avoid giving out signs that might be interpreted as boredom or irritation, such as drumming your fingers, tapping your feet, stifling a yawn, or looking at your watch?
- Did you avoid being distracted and letting your attention wander?
- Did you allow adequate pauses and avoid jumping in with your own ideas?
- Did you restrain yourself from completing sentences for the other person?
- Were you sure they had completed all that they wanted to say before you started speaking?
- Did you summarise what they had said to ensure that you understood?

Summary

1. Keep quiet and listen carefully.
2. Maintain eye contact as much as possible.
3. Give non-verbal acknowledgement – nods and smiles.
4. Use 'reflection' if silence is prolonged.
5. Rephrase and summarise to check understanding.
6. Use open questions – sparingly.

The beginning of wisdom is silence,
the next step is listening.

Zen Master

CHAPTER 7
Briefing

Description

Briefing is a tool used to pass important work-related information to your people. The information usually comes down through the organisation from senior management.

Background

Being at the first level of management, supervisors provide the link between the operational workforce and the management workforce. These are often referred to as 'the workforce' and 'management' respectively.

At one end of the chain, the responsibility of managers is to keep aware of the business and its wider environment, and to formulate goals and policies to keep the company healthy and the business profitable.

At the other end of the chain, the responsibility of the operational workforce is to do the operating work necessary to implement those goals and policies.

The responsibility of the supervisor is to manage the in-between stages as shown overleaf.

Supervisors
Identify operational objectives from strategic goals and communicate them to the workforce. Ensure that quality, time and budget targets are met.

Management
Keep aware of the business and its wider environment.

Formulate goals and policies.

Keep the company healthy and keep the business profitable.

Resolve strategic problems.

Workforce
Understand the objectives and operating tasks required to ensure achievement of the company's goals.

Perform their tasks safely and efficiently.

Resolve workface problems.

Resolve tactical problems.
Identify strategic problems from tactical ones, and communicate them to management.

At times, changes in goals, policies or procedures become necessary to ensure that the organisation stays healthy. Briefing is the tool used to communicate such changes from management to the workforce.

When to use briefing

- Whenever a new policy or procedure is introduced that affects your people.
- Whenever there are new safety regulations that may affect your people.
- Whenever there is a major change in objectives or targets.
- When you are asked by management to provide important information to your people.

How to use briefing

Step 1. Plan a suitable time and place
- Arrange a venue which is large enough for everyone, and as quiet and relaxed as possible.
- Ensure that everyone who needs to be there *can* be there.
- Ensure that everyone will be able to hear what you are saying.
- If you use visual aids, ensure everyone will be able to see them properly.
- Ensure that everyone can get there, and that everyone has the necessary travel passes, security passes, etc.
- Ensure that everyone knows where and when, and how to get there.

Step 2. Prepare the information carefully
- Ensure that you understand exactly what the brief is about. If you don't, postpone the briefing until you get clarification.
- Use visual aids if necessary. A diagram or a few key words on a flipchart can often help considerably.
- Do a 'trial run.' Present the information to someone you know and trust beforehand, and ask for their comments. (This often also helps to improve confidence.)

Step 3. Welcome everyone and set the groundrules
- Welcome everyone, using people's names as much as possible.

- Explain how long the briefing is expected to last and how it will be conducted.
- Make it clear at the beginning exactly when you will take questions. This prevents interruption by questions that may be answered later anyway.
- Make agreements about cigarette smoking that are acceptable to both smokers and non-smokers.

Step 4. Start with a short overview
- In one sentence, tell those present what the briefing is about. (For example, 'Following an inquiry into the XRD2 scheme, a new policy will be introduced next month'.) Be concise and specific.

Step 5. Present the information, keeping the message short and straightforward
- If the briefing is long or complex, present the information in smaller items. After each item, take one or two questions and then carry on to the next item.
- Summarise often.

Step 6. Invite and answer questions for clarification only
- Ensure that you only discuss questions that are relevant to the subject of the briefing. This can be difficult, as people tend to bring up their own current concerns, which may not be related. On the other hand, they are important, so make a note of them, and deal with them separately. (For example, 'Ken, that's an important point but it isn't relevant to this briefing ... I'll make a note of it and we can discuss it later. ... Now, are there any other questions?')

Step 7. Close the discussion with a summary

Step 8. Hand out any support material that may be required, and thank everyone for coming

Checklist for effective use

- Did you set groundrules concerning discussion and questions?
- Did you keep it short and straightforward?
- Did you avoid any false promises?
- Did you avoid making adverse comments?
- Did you stick to the point?
- Did you keep questions and discussion to the point?
- Did you maintain loyalty upwards?
- Did you maintain loyalty downwards?
- Did you say when you didn't know the answer to a question, rather than attempt to answer it?
- Did you ask questions to ensure that everyone understood?

Summary

1. Plan.
2. Prepare.
3. Welcome everyone.
4. Give an overview.
5. Present the information.
6. Clarify where necessary.
7. Summarise.
8. Close.

CHAPTER 8
Supervisory Meetings

Description

A work meeting consists of a group of people who have come together to reach a decision by discussion. Conducting a meeting ('chairing') is a co-ordinating tool to ensure the most effective use of time at a work meeting.

Background

A meeting is a collection of people who get together for the purpose of discussing an issue or problem. Different meetings have different purposes. In general, meetings that are conducted by supervisors at work may have one of two purposes: to pass on and discuss information coming down through the organisation from management (an *information meeting*, or *briefing*); or to make a decision about an issue or problem (a *decision-making meeting*). The objective of the person conducting the meeting (usually referred to as the Chair) is to achieve fully the purpose of the meeting.

Conducting an information meeting is dealt with in Chapter 7. This chapter deals with the supervisory skill of conducting a decision-making meeting, which is the type of meeting usually meant when we simply talk about *a meeting*.

The differences between a decision-making meeting and a briefing are given on the next page.

	Meeting	Briefing
Purpose	Making effective decisions	Passing on information
Communication flow	All directions	From top downwards
Function of participants	Contribute experience and expertise to the discussion	Listen to and understand the message
Function of the Chair	Involve everyone in the discussion and get synergy	Ensure everyone clearly understands the message
Seating arrangements	So everyone can see and hear everyone else	So everyone can see and hear the leader
Questions allowed	Clarifying, challenging, probing, what ... if ..., etc	Clarification only
End point	Action decisions	Message received
Type of interaction	Leader participating, from a position of equal status	Leader telling, from a position of authority

When to use a decision-making meeting

- Whenever a problem or issue arises that significantly affects the achievement of operational or project goals by your team.
- Whenever a problem or issue arises that significantly affects the effectiveness or morale of your team.
- When you are asked by management to make a decision on an issue or problem, and you believe that other people should be involved in the decision-making.
- Whenever you feel you need special help or support in making a decision.

How to conduct a meeting

Decision-making meetings have three distinct phases, each of which requires consideration:

Phase 1. Planning and preparation
Phase 2. The meeting itself
Phase 3. Following through

Phase 1. Planning and preparation

Step 1.1. Prepare yourself for the meeting
- Ensure that you understand exactly what the problem or issue is (your reason for calling the meeting), and what sort of decision you want to be made at the meeting (decisions on options and/or decisions for action).

Step 1.2. Plan to have the right people there – no more and no less
- Think about who should be at the meeting. Include people who have significant information, significant influence, or significant skills.
- Avoid leaving out significant people simply because you don't like them, and avoid including insignificant people because you like them.
- Arrange for someone to take notes of important points and decisions, and for someone to keep an eye on the time.

Step 1.3. Plan a suitable time and place
- Arrange a venue which suits everyone. If there is someone who should be present but cannot get there, think of other possibilities, such as arranging a formal teleconference.
- Ensure beforehand that everyone knows exactly what the meeting is about, and exactly why they are required to be there.
- Ensure that everyone will be able to hear what everyone else is saying.
- Make visual aids available, such as flipcharts or whiteboards – these often help to display information or decisions.
- Ensure everyone will be able to see any visual aids properly.
- Make a tape recorder available if possible – it can help the note taker, and is often useful for brainstorming.

- Ensure that everyone can get to the meeting, and that they have the necessary travel passes, security passes, etc.
- Ensure that everyone knows where and when the meeting will be held.

Phase 2. The meeting itself

Step 2.1. Welcome everyone and set the groundrules
- Welcome everyone, using people's names as much as possible.
- Explain how long the meeting will last, how it will be conducted, and what visual and auditory aids are available.
- Make acceptable agreements about cigarette smoking, breaks and question times.

Step 2.2. Start with a short overview
- Shortly and simply, make it clear at the beginning exactly what the issue is, and what you want to come out of the meeting.
- If the problem or issue is complicated, clarify it in smaller items. After each, answer any questions and then carry on to the next item.
- Check that everyone understands what the problem or issue is.

Step 2.3. Invite discussion in a planned sequence, wherever possible encouraging the quietest people first
- *Start with an analysis of the issue or problem*
  —Focus the discussion initially on facts and information from people's experience. Start with questions such as, 'Who knows anything about this problem?' or 'What do we actually know about this problem so far?'
  —Then focus on possible underlying problems or deeper issues. Ask questions such as, 'What could be behind this problem?' or 'What could be the underlying causes of this problem?' or 'What part of this problem are we not seeing?'

—Avoid moving on to trying to find solutions until no one has anything more to say on possible causes and underlying or contributory factors.

—Summarise often.

● *Move on to generating possible options for solving the problem*

—Get as many options as possible before starting to consider them. Use *brainstorming* if necessary. (Remember to ask the quieter people for their ideas first.)

● *Then focus on making a decision*

—Focus the discussion on which of the options are possible and practical.

—Once decisions are made, be sure to clarify exactly *who* will be responsible for doing *what* by *when*.

—Ensure that the decisions, actions and responsibilities are written down.

Step 2.4. Attend to the proper ending of the meeting

● Summarise the discussion, and the decisions taken.

● Ask for, and listen to, feedback about how you conducted the meeting. This will help you to learn how to improve your meetings.

● Thank everyone for coming.

Phase 3. The follow-through

● Send out the meeting notes or minutes, what was decided and what action will be taken by whom.

● Record the actions you have agreed to take, and ensure that you do them.

● Make a note in your diary or work planner to follow up on actions that were agreed by other members of your team.

Checklist for effective use – 1. Chair

● Was there a clear purpose for holding the meeting?

● Did you select the participants carefully?

● Did you prepare yourself for the meeting?

● Did you let everyone know well beforehand exactly what the meeting was about?

- Did you arrive early enough to check your arrangements and handle any last-minute problems?
- Did you start the meeting promptly at the arranged time?
- Did you elicit everyone's participation, including the quiet ones?
- Did you maintain proper control of the discussion, and keep everyone to the point?
- Did you summarise the decisions at the end of the meeting, and clarify all action to be taken? (What? Who? By when?)
- Did you request feedback from participants on how you conducted the meeting?
- Did you ensure that everyone received a copy of the meeting notes or minutes?
- Did you afterwards take the actions you agreed to?
- Did you follow up on the actions agreed by other members of your team?
- Did you leave the venue as tidy as you found it?

Checklist for effective use – 2. Participant

- Did you ensure you knew the purpose of the meeting beforehand?
- Did you ensure you had a reason to attend before agreeing?
- Did you confirm that you would be attending?
- Did you prepare yourself for the meeting, and bring what you needed with you?
- Did you arrive in good time?
- Did you ask questions when you were not clear about something?
- Did you listen to the ideas of others without interruption?
- Were you open to the ideas of others?
- Did you participate when you had something to contribute, and keep quiet when you had nothing to say?
- Did you help others stay on the subject?
- Did you give helpful feedback to the chairperson (by note or phone call)?
- Did you take the agreed action after the meeting?
- Did you inform appropriate people (who did not attend) about what was decided and agreed at the meeting?
- Did you avoid engaging in side conversations while the meeting was in progress?
- Did you attend the entire meeting and avoid leaving for non-emergency reasons?

Summary

Phase 1. Planning and preparation
- Prepare yourself.
- Invite the right people.
- Find the right time and place.

Phase 2. The meeting itself
- Welcome all and set groundrules.
- Give a short overview.
- Maintain an orderly discussion:
    defining the problem;

     analysing the problem;
     generating possible solutions;
     deciding on the best solution;
     allocating responsibilities.
- Summarise the decisions and actions.
- Learn from the experience.

Phase 3. Following through
- Confirm in writing.
- Take the action you agreed to.
- Check that others take action.

The anatomy of any organisation includes four different kinds of bones:
- Wish-bones — who wish someone else would do the work.
- Jaw-bones — who talk a lot but do little else.
- Knuckle-bones — who knock what everyone else does.
- Back-bones — who get down and actually do the work.
William Wilkerson

CHAPTER 9
Coaching

Description

Coaching with SDL (safety-centred discovery learning) is a method of coaching based on the principles of learning by discovery, with appropriate attention to the safety of people and equipment.

Background

People learn better if they discover things for themselves. Adults, in particular, don't like to be told what to do as if they were children. There is also no doubt that the challenge of finding something out for oneself is much more stimulating than having everything explained before getting 'hands on' experience.

On the other hand, many tasks that people need to learn to do may be associated with a real risk to the safety of themselves, other people, or the equipment. Allowing people to learn by discovery would be unethical in such situations.

By careful attention to how we use this tool (coaching with SDL), we can get the benefits of learning by doing, while ensuring that no harm comes to the learner, the equipment, or other people.

When to use coaching with SDL

Coaching with SDL is used to develop the skills of our people whenever we find that they are unable to perform a task, yet are willing and eager to do it.

Prerequisites for using coaching with SDL are:
- The person is unable to perform the task required of them due to lack of training or experience, and not due to physical incapability or disability.
- The person is eager and willing to learn. (If they are unwilling, some problem-identification and problem-solving is needed first.)

How to use coaching with SDL

Step 1. Outline the objective of the task clearly, without mentioning any of the steps in the process

This means telling the person what outcome is required, what ultimately has to be achieved. (For example, 'What you need to learn to do is to change the bulb inside this piece of equipment so that, when the power cable is plugged in and switched on the light comes on again.') Ensure that they understand the objective by asking for feedback.

Step 2. Carefully explain any safety factors involved in the activity and their implications

For example, 'The power supply is 230 volts – that's high enough to kill a person.' 'The bulb should not be touched with your fingers because the sweat on your hands can cause it to be damaged at high operating temperatures.' 'The lens under the cover is very fragile and can break easily.' 'The reflector must not be touched – it's highly polished.' 'If anything touches the drum, it will have to be replaced – at a cost of £85.' 'Anything inside the cover which is painted red will be hot enough to burn you if you touch it.' Ensure the safety factors and their implications are clearly understood.

Step 3. Allow the learner to carry on and work out, by trial and error, how to do the task

Watch carefully. Only give assistance when asked, and even then give as little as possible; rather encourage the learner to persist. Give positive feedback and encouragement when they do something right; if they make a mistake, just keep quiet and watch carefully. ('Don't just do something, stand there!')

Step 4. Intervene immediately if they are about to do something unsafe

Have a pre-arranged signal to make them stop. Usually, it just needs an agreement that, as soon as you say, 'Stop!' they will stop immediately, and look to you for advice. Explain the safety hazard and let them continue.

Step 5. Once the learner has successfully completed the task, invite any questions and discuss them

This allows the learner to fill in anything they don't understand.

Step 6. Ask the learner to summarise the steps

Step 7. Ask them to complete the whole process once more without any assistance at all

This allows for their learning and confidence to be consolidated.

Checklist for effective use

● Was he or she willing and eager to learn to do the task?
● Are you sure they understand *what* is to be achieved – the outcome objective?
● Did you avoid telling them *how* to do it?
● Were you sure they understood all the safety factors?
● Did you resist telling them what to do just because they seemed frustrated?
● Were you patient and pleasant throughout?
● Did you give them occasional encouragement and support?

- Did you save discussion until after they had completed the task?
- Did you ensure their safety at all times?
- Did you resist intervening too early or if they took too long?
- Did you avoid criticising?
- Were you patient throughout, even if they seemed to take too long?

Summary

When to use coaching with SDL

Appropriate coaching with SDL	Inappropriate coaching with SDL
• The person does not have the necessary ability, training and experience to do the task.	• The person already has the ability, training and experience to do the task.
• The person is willing and eager to do the task.	• The person is unwilling to do the task.
• The person is physically able to perform the activities required to do the task.	• The person is physically incapacitated or disabled in relation to the particular task.

How to coach with SDL
1. Explain the result required. Check understanding.
2. Explain safety aspects. Check understanding.
3. Leave them alone — watch carefully to control safety. Encourage them to find out for themselves. Intervene immediately if safety is at risk.
4. On completion, invite questions.
5. Summarise and repeat once more.

Leader or Boss?

The Boss drives the work team.
The Leader inspires them.

The Boss depends on authority.
The Leader depends on goodwill.

The Boss evokes fear.
The Leader radiates respect.

The Boss says 'I'.
The Leader says 'We'.

The Boss shows who is wrong.
The Leader shows what is wrong.

The Boss knows how it is done.
The Leader knows how to do it.

The Boss demands respect.
The Leader commands respect.

So be a Leader,
Not a Boss.

From a wall in a government office in Harare

CHAPTER 10
Monitoring Performance

Description

Monitoring is the tool we use when we keep a regular check on the performance of our people and to determine whether it is up to standard.

Background

In order to determine whether someone is performing to an acceptable standard, we need first to observe what they are doing, or have done. Only then can we make a judgement on their performance.

The purpose for the supervisor to monitor someone's performance is important to bear in mind, as monitoring can become associated with 'policing' or 'spying'. In constructive monitoring, the supervisor is neither a policeman nor a spy, but a prospector looking for gold. We check performance to discover what the employee is doing well (the real nuggets) and what is not being done to standard.

To know what they are doing well provides us with many opportunities. It gives us an idea of their talents and experience. Knowing these, we can use them constructively when we plan and organise other tasks. It gives us an opportunity to express appreciation and praise. It identifies areas of expertise that may be used to train other people who don't have the same skills.

Everyone in an organisation acts as a link in a larger chain — knowing where people are not performing to standard provides us with the opportunity to take corrective action quickly, so that further links in the chain are not adversely affected. When we do find substandard performance, we need to do something about it — this is dealt with in Chapter 11.

In reality, most people are continually monitoring their own performance. Once they know and understand what standards are expected of them, the majority of people know whether or not they are doing a proper job, and will seek assistance if they are not managing. As supervisors, our function is to ensure that this is happening, and to identify situations where, for some reason or another, the person is unable to recognise, or is unwilling to seek assistance for, substandard performance.

Monitoring encompasses a wide range of checking activities. At one end of the spectrum is the 'annual appraisal', which is often a formal process with a well-defined procedure. At the other end of the spectrum is a quick informal process lasting a minute or two. While the timing, the formality and the amount of record-keeping may differ across the spectrum, the principles remain the same. The focus of this chapter, however, is the day-to-day monitoring that is one of the main tools of the supervisor's job.

Monitoring involves observing and judging the general work behaviour of each of our people, as well as each of their tasks. The same person may require one of their tasks to be monitored frequently and other tasks to be monitored only very occasionally. This means we need to give some thought to how we monitor each person's performance in relation to each of their tasks.

Indications for increasing the frequency of monitoring
- The person is inexperienced in the task and has never done anything similar.
- The task carries a high degree of risk or danger.
- The person expresses lack of confidence (for example, after sick leave).

- The person's performance of the task is deteriorating for any reason.

Indications for reducing the frequency of monitoring
- The person's performance of the task shows a steady improvement.
- The person shows willingness and ability in performing the task.
- The person shows that they are able to monitor their own performance and seek assistance readily.

How to monitor performance

Monitoring performance involves observing indicators of performance, and comparing them with a defined standard. Sometimes people exceed the standards required of them, sometimes their performance is 'satisfactory', and sometimes it is substandard. *If no standards of performance have been set, we cannot even begin to monitor performance.* The most frustrating supervisors and managers are those who do not set (or communicate) standards of performance, and thus their people only find out that they have 'done wrong' *after* they have done it. Failure of a supervisor to ensure that their people understand the standards expected of them is inexcusable.

Monitoring = Observing + Judging
Judging = Comparing with standards expected

Step 1. Ensure beforehand that they know what the standards are
The standards of a task or job describe what will be checked or measured to ensure that the job has been done properly. It always involves checking the output (the result of doing the task) and often also involves checking the procedure used. (Agreeing on standards is part of start-up induction and mutual objective setting as described in Chapters 2 and 3.)

Step 2. Agree how each task will be checked

Once people know what standards are expected of them, the easiest way to overcome any resistance to checking what they are doing is to involve them in deciding how their work will be checked, and how often.

Discuss what observations will be made, where and by whom. Use the indications above to discuss how often. Small item outputs and documents such as reports can be brought to you for checking. At other times you may need to go to them.

Step 3. Make observations – and record them if necessary

'Making observations' means seeing for yourself, and not relying on hearsay. Use your feet. Get around. It is useful to visit the workplace of all employees occasionally, as this creates extra opportunities to observe their performance, to observe good ideas they may be using, or to talk about potential problems before they become an issue. Don't arrive unannounced unless you have cleared that with them beforehand.

Use your eyes and ears. Concentrate on things you can see, count or measure. Keep the standards in mind while you are observing.

On major tasks, keep a record of your observations – they could be important for someone working towards a qualification or promotion, or for comparison later if their performance changes. Record only what you can see, count or measure. Avoid making judgements until *after* you have made all your observations.

Step 4. Make your judgements

Compare your observations with the agreed standards. Note where the observed performance matches the standards, exceeds the standards or falls short of them.

Step 5. Take action

Performance that is up to standard should be recognised and acknowledged. It is important for your people to know that you know they are doing a good job. Performance that exceeds the expected standards may also need to be rewarded. This will depend on the policies and practices of your organisation. In general, it pays never to miss an opportunity to reward superior performance.

Substandard performance needs to be challenged and corrected. How to do this is dealt with in the next chapter.

It is a good idea to make notes of the action you take in response to monitoring your people's performance, because it is an indication of *your* performance.

Checklist for effective use

- Do all your people know the standards expected of them, in terms of general work behaviour?
- Do all your people know the objectives and standards for each of their key tasks?
- Are you sure that everyone is clear how their work will be monitored?
- Do you avoid gut reactions and snap judgements?
- Do you *always* give appreciation and praise when it is due?
- Do you always take action when someone's performance is not up to standard?
- Are you sure that *all* your people know how you think they are performing?

Summary

Monitoring = Observing + Judging

1. Clarify the standards.
2. Agree how work will be checked.
3. Make regular observations.
4. Judge against standards.
5. Take action.

Note 1. It is important to emphasise that we are monitoring employees' *performance*, we are not here to make judgements on their *motives* or their *qualities* as people.

Note 2. Spending some time on getting your high performers to perform even better may have a higher pay-off than spending too much time on the problems of your low performers. Keep them all in balance.

CHAPTER 11
Challenging Substandard Performance

Description

Challenging substandard performance is a response to your judgement that someone is not performing as they agreed to, or are expected to. It is a communication tool used to give feedback and start solving problems. Its purpose is to move the person's performance back up to standard, while enabling you to maintain a positive relationship with them.

Background

An essential part of your function as supervisor is to maintain the performance of your people at a high level. You cannot do this alone — you also need their co-operation.

During the planning phase, we look forward with our people, decide what they will do, and define how well it needs to be done — we set objectives and define performance standards. At times, we check how things are going and make a judgement as to whether they are going according to plan. This is referred to as our *monitoring* function.

When we find that someone's performance is up to standard or exceeds the standards set, we respond with praise and acknowledgement of a job well done. When we find that their performance is not what was expected and agreed to, we have a problem. A problem exists when there is a difference between the way things are and the way someone wants them to be. We can use CSP (challenging substandard performance) as the tool for working on the person's performance. It is the spokeshave we use for trimming off the rough edges.

Here it is important to note that it is not the *person* that is the problem, but their *performance*. There is a big difference between regarding *Bill* as a problem, and regarding Bill's *performance* as a problem. Think about it. If we regard Bill as a problem, we have to tackle Bill. But if we regard Bill's performance as a problem, we can tackle the problem *with* Bill. It is no longer us against Bill, it is Bill and us against the problem of substandard performance.

When to challenge substandard performance

● Whenever you observe that someone's performance is inadequate, it should be challenged.

How to challenge substandard performance

Step 1. State your criticism as a problem or concern
Start with a general statement of concern. ('John, I'm concerned that we may have a problem.') Next, tell them two things: what you have observed; and in what way this does not come up to the standards. ('I see that you are not wearing your safety goggles. Our health and safety regulations state that we must wear them whenever we do any welding.') Keep the focus on facts, not on feelings at this stage.

Step 2. State the reason for your concern
Explain what the possible outcomes of their behaviour may be, both for themselves and for others. ('The reason for my concern is that your eyes may be damaged by the UV light. Even if the damage is only temporary, it means that you will be off work, which places more strain on the others.') Still keep the focus on facts.

Step 3. State your wants or requirements clearly

Usually this means restating their standards of performance relevant to this particular situation. ('I'd like you to wear your safety goggles every time without exception, and to keep them on all the time you are welding.')

Step 4. State the positive consequences

Explain the positive consequences of up-to-standard performance. ('By always wearing your goggles, you'll not only ensure your eyes are protected, you'll also keep us both out of trouble if the boss happens to come in.')

Step 5. Check that they have understood what you said

In order to be sure they have understood you, ask them to repeat, in their own words, what you have told them.

Step 6. Ask for, and listen to their response

Now you can start to respond to their feelings by asking open questions. ('How do you feel about this?') As they reply to you, listen carefully using the tool of active listening. Usually, that is all that is required.

Step 7. Move on to problem-solving if necessary

Occasionally, the substandard performance is due to factors of which we were unaware, or over which the person has no control. In this case, we move on to problem-solving, using one of the problem-solving tools. The main thing to remember here is not to let any secondary problem at this stage divert you from the primary problem, which is their substandard performance. Keep in mind, and remind them, that the secondary problem does not excuse them from their responsibilities. Keep it clear that, in addition to any action taken on the problems they may be having, you expect them to maintain the standards required (as stated in step 3.) Then move on to solving the secondary problem.

Checklist for effective use

- Did you clearly state the *observations* on which you made your judgement?
- Did you discuss only the person's *behaviour* (what they did or didn't *do*, not what they *are* or are not)?
- Did you carefully avoid referring to the person's attitude?
- Did you make clear the reason for the expected standard of performance?
- Did you make clear how their performance differed from what was expected?
- Were you very specific about what you require them to do?
- Did you avoid general statements such as 'pull your socks up' or 'improve your attitude'?
- Did you avoid being side-tracked by the secondary problem until after the response to the primary one was completed?
- Did you avoid 'bringing up' past problems in the present situation?

Summary

1. State your criticism as a problem or concern.
2. State the reason for your concern.
3. State your wants or requirements clearly.
4. State the positive consequences.
5. Check that they have understood.
6. Ask for, and listen to, their response.
7. Move into problem-solving if necessary.

Zymurgy's Law: When it hits the fan, it's never distributed equally.

CHAPTER 12
Critical Incident Learning

Description

Critical incident learning is a technique for learning from an incident in which things have gone wrong. It is based on an adult learning cycle, and provides an alternative to the common response of simply finding someone to blame.

Background

A critical incident, in this sense, means an incident in which things have not gone according to plan. By learning from such incidents, we can make the best of a potentially bad situation in three ways:

(a) We can ensure that the problem doesn't recur.
(b) We can increase our skills and understanding.
(c) We can earn the respect of our people by getting the best out of a potentially bad situation.

The adult learning cycle consists of reflecting on an incident (the critical incident) in three structured phases, based on three key questions: 'What?', 'So what?', and 'Now what?'

Key question	Examples	Time focus	Purpose
What?	What happened? What did you see? What time was it? Who was there? etc.	**Past** Looking back	To focus attention objectively on what happened, and separate the facts from assumptions.
So what?	So what does all this mean? So what can we conclude from all this? So what can we learn from what happened?	**Present** Looking into, around and underneath	To understand the sequence of how things happened, and find links between causes and effects.
Now what?	What can we possibly do to improve things in future? What can we do to prevent this happening again?	**Future** Looking forward	To generate ideas, and decide on what changes need to be made in future.

When to use critical incident learning

- Whenever anyone (including yourself) makes a mistake.
- Whenever you find yourself blaming someone because things are not going according to plan, or have gone wrong.

How to use critical incident learning

Step 1. Ask, 'What happened?' and listen actively
Don't make any assumptions, ask questions instead. Don't

move to the next step until you are sure that both you and the employee have a clear picture of exactly what happened.

Step 2. Ask, 'So what can be learned from that?' and facilitate their learning

This step may require patience on your part, because people often expect you (as the supervisor) to provide the answers. It is worth waiting silently until they start to put their learning into words. Encouragement, in the form of saying things such as, 'Good, what else?' or 'Yes, and ... ?' can also help. Once again, avoid being in a hurry to move to the next step.

Step 3. Ask, 'What will you do differently next time?' and facilitate their action decisions

Often people will state general action *ideas* at this stage, such as 'I need to communicate better'. Encourage them to be specific about action decisions — exactly *who* they will communicate with, *how* they will communicate with them, exactly *when*, and so on.

Step 4. Summarise

Once you have worked through the learning cycle (What? So what? Now what?), summarise the main points of their learning and action decisions. This helps to fix them in your mind, and also makes it clear to the person that you have listened and understood what they have said.

Practical hints

- If you are angry or frustrated about what happened, take a short break before getting into this discussion.
- Whenever you ask a question, make sure you *listen* to the answers.
- If the person seems to 'dry up' after a question, just say '... and?' or '... and then?' and wait quietly. Once they understand you really want to listen to what they have to say, they will start talking.
- Take plenty of time for this sort of discussion. It will save a

lot more time in future.
- Don't fly off the handle before you have heard everything they have to say (by then, you probably won't have to).

Checklist for effective use

- Did you give enough time to this discussion?
- Did you outline to them the reason for the discussion?
- Did you complete each phase adequately?
- Did you spend more time listening than talking (even in phase 3)?
- Did you hear them out without interruption?
- In phase 1, did you clearly separate facts from assumptions and opinions?
- In phase 2, did you give them enough time and encouragement to identify all that could be learned from the situation?
- Did you learn something new yourself?
- In phase 3, did you give them enough time and encouragement to identify at least four or five possible options before deciding on any?
- Did you avoid hurrying or appearing to be in a hurry?
- Did you avoid dragging other incidents or past complaints into the discussion?

God gave us two ears and one mouth — perhaps the intention was that we should use them in that proportion.

Philemon Raphunga, Foreman

Summary

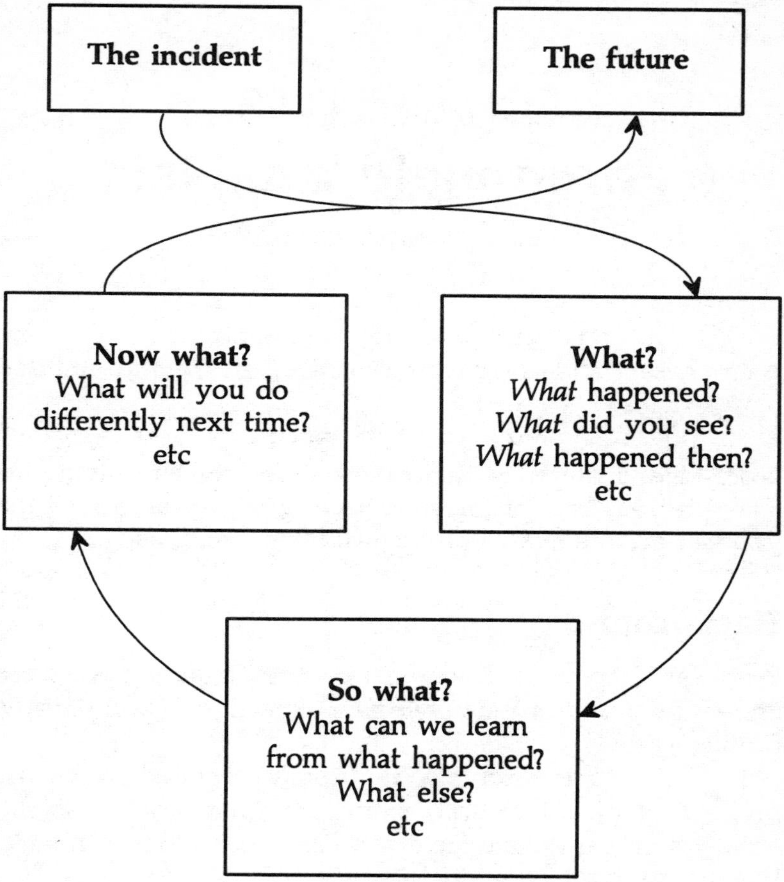

The critical incident learning cycle

CHAPTER 13
Force-Field Analysis

Description

Force-field analysis is a tool used in problem-solving for analysing the field of forces impacting on a problem, so that you can make effective problem-solving decisions.

Background

Problems may be considered as either requiring a correct answer (logical problem-solving) or a creative answer (creative problem-solving).

Logical problem-solving is usually required when the problem is of a technical nature. Creative problem-solving usually involves human factors or complex situations in which there is no 'right or wrong' answer.

Force-field analysis, first described by Kurt Lewin in a book called *The Planning of Change* (Holt, Rinehart & Winston, 1989), is a tool that helps us to tackle such problems in a systematic way.

When to use force-field analysis

- It can be used in any creative problem-solving situation, and is especially useful when human dynamics are involved.
- It is suitable for use by individuals or groups, and is

particularly useful for quality improvement teams or quality circles, that is, groups of people with shared work backgrounds who voluntarily meet on a regular basis to investigate, analyse and solve their work-related problems.

How to use force-field analysis

Force-field analysis is conducted in three steps (see the worksheet on p. 71).

Step 1. Define the problem in a particular way
Define the problem by describing two situations: the situation as it is now, and the situation as it would be if ideal. The goal of the problem-solving activity then becomes clear — to move the 'situation now' towards the 'situation ideal'.

Step 2. List the *helping* and *hindering* forces
Begin by listing all the factors in the situation that are *helping* it to move from 'now' to 'ideal'. Be very specific. Consider factors such as equipment, facilities, systems, procedures and people. When considering people factors, list exactly who is doing exactly what.

Then make a list of all the factors in the situation that are *hindering* the move from 'now' to 'ideal'. Again, be very specific, listing what equipment is faulty or unavailable, what facilities are needed but not available, which systems or procedures are blocking, and who is doing what to hinder progress.

Finally, arrange the lists in order of priority, putting the factors having the most impact at the top of the list.

Step 3. Focus planning on the *hindering* factors only
Starting from the top of the list, make a specific plan to remove each of the hindering factors. Ignore the helping factors — they are working for you already, so concentrate on the task of getting the hindering factors out of the way.

In complex problem situations, some of the hindering factors may require a separate force-field analysis of their own.

Checklist for effective use

- Does the problem being considered require a creative answer rather than a logical one?
- Has the problem been defined in terms of the situation-as-now and the situation-as-ideal?
- Are the helping forces on your list all factors that actually exist, and are *not* 'could helps', 'should helps' or 'would helps'?
- Are the hindering forces on your list all factors that are actually hindering (not 'could hinders')?
- If people are involved in your lists, are they accurately identified?
- Are the people factors listed in terms that describe specific behaviours (observable actions)?
- Have you made a definite plan to remove all the major hindering factors?
- Do your plans contain a description of definite action steps to be taken, with deadlines for each, and an indication of what help may be required?

Force-Field Analysis Worksheet

Situation as *now*	→	Situation as *ideal*

Helping factors	Hindering factors
→	←

	Plans to remove hindering factors
1.	
2.	
3.	
4.	
5.	
6.	

CHAPTER 14
Decision Grids

Description

Decisions are choices of action that you make during planning or problem-solving activities. Decision grids are tools that can help you to make more effective choices during the decision-making process.

Background

When we make a decision, we seem to start by simply making a choice. When we say, 'We have decided what to do', what we seem to be saying is, in fact, 'Of all the things we *could* do, this is the one that we *will* do'. So, in addition to making a choice about what we do, a decision is often also a statement of intent.

It sometimes happens that, because of the pressure on us at work, we decide what to do because it seems to be the quickest or easiest way to sort out the issue immediately, and then find later that some other course of action would have been more effective. We look back and regret that we didn't give it more thought before acting.

Using a decision grid can help us to sort out our thoughts while we are making a decision. It can help us to be sure that we have considered the situation in a logical way, and have not simply just responded to the pressure of the situation. We need to remember that decision grids help us to make a choice about what to do – they don't help us to do it ... that we have to do for ourselves.

This chapter describes three of the most commonly used decision grids, namely:

1. Comparison of paired alternatives
2. Weighting and rating grid
3. Bi-directional ranking matrix.

They are described below and examples are shown on the following pages.

When to use which decision grid

- When we are faced with having to make a choice from a fairly large number of options, an effective grid to use is *comparison of paired alternatives.*
- When we are faced with having to make a choice from a smaller number of options, but there are a large number of referent criteria, an effective grid to use is the *weighting and rating grid.*
- When we are faced with having to make a choice from a medium number of options (three to five) and have a medium number of referent criteria (four or five), an effective grid to use is the *bi-directional ranking matrix.*

How to use decision grid 1

Comparison of paired alternatives

Step 1. List all the options available and label them alphabetically (A, B, C, etc)

Step 2. Write down your referent criteria
These can be thought of as the questions you will ask yourself when deciding between the options. They are the values or constraints on which you will be making your decision. The three most common referent criteria for decisions at work are:
● most effective?
● most practical and realistic?
● most economic?

Step 3. Make a grid as indicated in the diagram opposite

Step 4. Compare each pair of options and circle the option that most fulfils the referent criteria

Step 5. Add up the ringed options; the highest number indicates the highest ranking

Decision grid 1: Comparison of paired alternatives

	Option A	A B	A C	A D	A E	A F	A G	A H	A I	A J
	Option B	B C	B D	B E	B F	B G	B H	B I	B J	
	Option C	C D	C E	C F	C G	C H	C I	C J		
	Option D	D E	D F	D G	D H	D I	D J			
	Option E	E F	E G	E H	E I	E J				
	Option F	F G	F H	F I	F J					
	Option G	G H	G I	G J						
	Option H	H I	H J							
	Option I	I J								
	Option J									

Option	A	B	C	D	E	F	G	H	I	J
Number of responses										

How to use decision grid 2

The weighting and rating grid

Step 1. Label the possible options (A, B, C, etc)

Step 2. List all the referent criteria (a, b, c, etc)

These are the factors that need to be considered when deciding between the options. They are the values and/or constraints on which you will be making your decision.

Step 3. Give each referent criterion a weighting of 1 to 5 based on importance

Step 4. Make a grid as indicated in the diagram opposite

Step 5. Write down a rating for each option in the grid boxes

This is done by rating the degree to which each option fulfils the referent criteria on a scale of 1 to 5, with $1 =$ low and $5 =$ high. Write the ratings in the left-hand section of each box.

Step 6. Score out your ratings

Multiply the number in each box by the weight-rating for that referent, and write the score in the right-hand section of each box. Then total the right-hand columns downwards.

Step 7. The highest total indicates the top priority

Decision grid 2: The weighting and rating grid

Referent criteria	Assigned weighting	Option A		Option B		Option C		Option D		Option E	
		R	Sc	R	Sc	R	Sc	R	Sc	R	Sc
a											
b											
c											
d											
e											
f											
g											
hi											
j											
etc											

Totals ☐ ☐ ☐ ☐ ☐

How to use decision grid 3

Bi-directional ranking matrix

Step 1. List the possible options and label them alphabetically (A, B, C, etc)

Step 2. List the referent criteria, and rank them in order of importance
Rank the criterion you regard as most important 1, the next most important 2, etc.

Step 3. Make a grid as in the diagram opposite

Step 4. Consider the first referent criterion, and rank the options
Look at all the options with reference to criterion 'a'. Consider which option best fits that criterion. Rank it 1. Rank the next best fit 2 and so on until you have worked across all the options. Write these rankings in the left-hand section of each box. Then move to the next referent criterion.

Step 5. Consider each referent criterion in order, and write the rankings in the left-hand section of the appropriate boxes

Step 6. Multiply the number in each box by the referent ranking (step 2), and total the columns downwards

Step 7. The lowest total indicates the top priority

Decision grid 3: Bi-directional ranking matrix

Referent criteria	Ranking (r)	Option A		Option B		Option C		Option D		Option E	
		R	rxR	R	rxR	R	rxR	R	rxR	R	rxR
a											
b											
c											
d											
e											
Totals											

Checklist for effective use

- Ensure that all options are stated as clear and specific options for action.
- Spend time determining your referent criteria. They are an indication of your values and constraints.
- Ensure that everyone affected by the outcome of the decision is involved in determining the referent criteria.
- Avoid being a slave to decision grids. If they work for you, that's fine. If their outcome doesn't feel right, scrap it.
- Avoid using decision grids for show: don't waste time using a decision grid when you already know the decision.

Fitzmaurice's Law: When you come to a stop sign and can't decide whether to turn left or right, any decision will be wrong.

Fried's Third Law of Public Administration: If it's logical, rational, reasonable, and makes good common sense ... don't do it.

CHAPTER 15
Authority and Respect

Description

The two main sources of power that allow you to influence your people are authority and respect. Authority is the power to influence others that is given to you by the organisation when you are selected or promoted into a supervisory position. (It can be thought of as *the power of our position*.) Respect is the power to influence people that they themselves give — you cannot expect it, you have to earn it. (It can be thought of as *the power in a relationship*.)

Background

We need to be able to influence others if we are to be effective supervisors. Most of the human tools we use as supervisors depend on our ability to influence our people.

The word *influence* is derived from the Latin "fluere", 'to flow'. When we are influencing people, they are, so to speak, flowing with us. When our people are influenced because of our authority, they flow with us because they have to. When they are influenced because they respect us, they flow with us because they want to. This is not the 'respect' shown to bullies and dictators, which is inspired by fear. Rather, it is the respect built on admiration and trust and which has no fear attached to it. Our initial task as supervisors is to maintain the authority of our position, while building a relationship with our people based on respect and trust.

As we start to use the authority given to us as a supervisor, we invariably find our authority being 'tested' by our people, especially if we have previously been their workmates. They come late, they take short-cuts, they break the rules – they do all sorts of little things to see how we will respond. This can be annoying, but it is natural and normal, because what they are really testing, is to see whether they can trust and respect us. Our response to this *testing phase* will make or break their respect and trust in the future.

Pete's principles of authority:

1. Authority will always be tested.
2. No amount of authority can overcome distrust and disrespect.

When to maintain authority and build respect

- Whenever it's raining outside.
- Whenever it's not raining outside.

How to maintain authority and build respect

Building respect and trust can be thought of as building a stone bridge. Each stone has to be the right size and carefully placed, otherwise the whole thing will collapse. The following are the key principles (building stones) for building a bridge between authority and respect.

1. Apply all of the rules, all of the time, and be seen to do so
Keeping to established rules, policies and procedures can sometimes be difficult, especially during the testing phase. Your people may put you in a position where you have to choose between bending the rules and being popular with them.

Rules are made because of a specific reason at some time in the past. You don't always know why the rules were made, especially if you are new to the position. It may be better to find out more about a rule before flouting it or allowing your people to flout it. It is only when you know the reason behind it that you are able to judge it.

If a rule is unfair or unreasonable, ultimately you will gain more respect if you get the rule changed, than if you ignore or break it.

One response could be, 'I realise that the rule seems unreasonable, and I'm not sure why it was made. I'll find out more about it, but in the meantime I'd like us all to stick to it.' (Then see principle 2 about promises.)

2. Never make a promise you cannot keep, or an agreement you cannot stick to
The quickest way to make people lose trust in you is to make a promise and then not keep it. Your subordinates may put considerable pressure on you to make promises or agreements, especially if you are new. If you feel comfortable about making a promise, and are sure you can keep it, go ahead. If not, a possible response may be, 'It would be nice if I could agree to that, but I wouldn't like to. I don't know enough about the situation, and I'm not sure I could keep to any promises right now.' (Then look for other options to tackle the problem.)

Remember that there are certain times when you are most at risk of being trapped into making promises you don't really want to make:

- At the end of a meeting that has gone over time.
- When someone is leaving your office and stops at the door to say, 'Oh, by the way, I wonder if you could ... ?'
- When someone says, 'I hope you don't mind, but I told X that you would attend to ... '

3. Keep your people informed – and keep yourself informed
Most experienced supervisors know that everyone should be

kept informed of everything that is going on *that may have an effect on them*. In this way, possible problems may be identified at an early phase, when it is easier to do something about them. So tell them as soon as you know — don't wait until the last minute.

Keeping your people informed, however, also means giving them *information* — not rumour, not gossip, not half-baked truths, but clear concise information. To do this effectively, you need to keep yourself well informed. Talk to your manager. Read the company newspaper. Stay informed — and if you don't know, say so.

4. Maintain a 'hostility-free' work area
As a supervisor, you are at the forefront of the effort to eliminate prejudice and harassment from the workplace. It is easier in the long run to make your position clear right at the beginning:

- that you intend to maintain a workplace in which *everyone* feels at ease;
- that you would like *everyone* to avoid behaviour that causes offence, such as suggestive or racist jokes, leers and embarrassing comments, displaying offensive pictures or calendars, graffiti and so on.
- that, if a person is not sure whether their behaviour may be offensive or not, to ask themselves the following questions:
  —Would you say or do this in front of your spouse or parents?
  —Would you say or do this in front of a workmate of the same sex?
  —Would you mind if what you say or do appears in the newspaper?

5. Make your people special
After all, they are special. They are the people you rely on to get your job done. Making people feel special doesn't have to be expensive or patronising. It means, for instance, having a sectional logo, informally meeting with them (and them alone)

for coffee at a particular time regularly, finding opportunities to give them credit when it is due, and being sure you know their names and using their name when you speak to them.

Praise them in public, complain to them in private. Fight their corner at meetings. Treat them as individuals, but be firm and fair to all. When you make your people special, you become a special supervisor — and they will respect you as such.

Checklist for effective use of your authority

- Do you ensure that the rules are kept by everyone, at all times?
- Do you keep to the rules yourself?
- Do you treat everyone with equal strictness or politeness?
- Do you enforce the rules politely and courteously at all times?
- Are you firm and fair in your enforcement of rules and procedures?
- Do you avoid being pushed into making promises, especially when you are under pressure?
- Do you pass on information as soon as possible?
- Do you avoid passing on gossip and rumours?
- Do you clarify the truth behind rumours and gossip with your own manager or someone who really knows what is going on first?
- Do you know the name of everyone in your section or department?
- Do you avoid the temptation to tell sexist or racist jokes at work?
- Are you sure that *everyone* feels comfortable about the social work environment?
- Are you sure that *everyone* understands your position on prejudice and harassment?
- Have you made sure that you are fully informed about your company's policies and procedures concerning offensive behaviour?
- Are you approachable and even-tempered to everyone?

Summary

Keep them informed

Keep your promises		Keep out harassment

Keep to the rules		Keep them special

Authority		**Respect and trust**

CHAPTER 16
Maintaining Self-esteem

Description

Self-esteem refers to how good people feel about themselves. Maintaining your subordinates' self-esteem indicates your respect for them. This creates respect for you.

Background

Supporting a job on a workbench makes it easier for us to use other tools. For instance, imagine cutting a plank without using a workbench. In the same way, maintaining self-esteem provides a firm supporting structure for other supervisory tools.

A high self-esteem means that people feel good about themselves and what they are doing. With this internal support, they have a greater confidence, a positive attitude, a higher level of personal energy, and an increased ability to think accurately and act decisively. Without self-esteem, people have no internal support. Their ability to think and act may become erratic and unsteady.

Maintaining the self-esteem of everyone with whom we work will provide a workbench for every managerial task we perform, and for every managerial tool we use. And by maintaining the self-esteem of others, we increase our own. As our own self-esteem rises, it becomes easier to respond to others positively. Thus, self-esteem becomes self-perpetuating.

When to maintain self-esteem

Maintaining the self-esteem of people is an essential part of *every* supervisory interaction and should be used in *every* supervisory situation.

How to maintain self-esteem

Step 1. Identify your own esteem-building and toxic behaviour profile
Go through the two checklists on page 88, and assess your own behaviour. Make a tick in the box if you use the behaviour *often* or *always*. (By 'toxic' behaviour, we mean behaviour that damages self-esteem.)

Step 2. Consider your behaviour profile and make action decisions
Decide which esteem-building behaviours you want to increase, and which toxic behaviours you want to decrease.

Step 3. Review your behaviour profile regularly
Add to your esteem-building behaviours and work at removing your toxic behaviours on a regular basis. It helps to discuss your decisions with someone you know and trust, and ask them to give you feedback on your progress.

Summary

When our people feel good about themselves, they do a good job. When they do a better job, they feel better about themselves, so they do an even better job.

Maintaining our own self-esteem is an important part of maintaining the self-esteem of others.

Checklist for effective use

Esteem-building behaviour
- [ ] Smiling often
- [ ] Making eye contact with others
- [ ] Greeting others by name
- [ ] Praising and complimenting others sincerely
- [ ] Listening attentively; hearing the other person out
- [ ] Stating your own needs and desires honestly
- [ ] Challenging others constructively on difficult issues
- [ ] Asking straightforward, non-loaded questions
- [ ] Keeping the confidence of others; avoiding gossiping
- [ ] Keeping to your word if you give it
- [ ] Using humour constructively
- [ ] Expressing genuine interest in the other person
- [ ] Delaying automatic reactions; not flying off the handle easily.

Toxic behaviour
- [ ] Complaining or whining
- [ ] Ridiculing others
- [ ] Monopolising the conversation
- [ ] Criticising and finding fault with others
- [ ] Interrupting
- [ ] Losing your temper easily
- [ ] Failing to keep promises
- [ ] Joking at inappropriate times
- [ ] Asking loaded or accusing questions
- [ ] Using 'should' language; pushing others with words
- [ ] Soliciting approval from others excessively
- [ ] Evading honest questions; refusing to be straightforward with others.

The difference between a princess and a flower-girl ... is the way they're treated.

Henry Higgins in *Pygmalion*
by G B Shaw

CHAPTER 17
Progressive Relaxation

Description

Progressive relaxation is a quick and simple tool for 'destressing' — for relaxing both body and mind.

Background

In the pressure of day-to-day supervision, we sometimes find that our tension works against us. When this happens, it means that we are letting stress get to us. Progressive relaxation can help us through the block and get us moving again.

When to use progressive relaxation

- Whenever we want to think clearly, for example, when making important decisions.
- When we want to gather our thoughts after a tense meeting or incident.
- Before we go home (or on the way home) so that we can leave work behind.
- When we feel nervous, for example, before an interview.
- Whenever we are feeling tense or stressed.

How to use progressive relaxation

Step 1. Find a quiet place
Close your door or move to a place where you can be reasonably quiet.

Step 2. Get comfortable
Sit comfortably with your back supported (on the floor if necessary) with your head balanced comfortably, your legs uncrossed and your eyes gently closed. Loosen clothing if it feels tight.

Step 3. Relax your mind
Concentrate on breathing quietly and smoothly, and imagine yourself in the most peaceful place you know. Relax like this for a minute or two.

Step 4. Relax your body
While holding this peaceful state of mind, tense the muscles of your feet by curling your toes. Once you can feel their tension, let them relax completely and leave them relaxed. Then move up to your calves: tense the muscles, let them relax completely, and leave them relaxed. Progress on to your thighs, bottom, stomach, back, shoulders, arms, neck and face, using the same sequence — tense, relax, leave them relaxed. Complete your relaxation by tensing your eyes and mouth and relaxing them.

Step 5. Relax totally for a few minutes
Spend a few minutes in this heavy, totally relaxed state,

resting your mind by imagining you are in your most peaceful place.

Step 6. Move back to reality in a different gear
As you get moving again, remind yourself about the things you do well and about the people who love you. Devise a personal motto to help to remember this quietness of mind in your work.

Checklist for effective use

- Do you avoid making excuses for not relaxing, such as, 'There's no place to go' or 'I'm too busy'?
- Do you occasionally remind yourself of the following:
  —Nothing lasts forever.
  —I've always made it up to now – I'll make it again.
  —I'm not alone in this.
  —Success is getting what I want; happiness is wanting what I get.
  —Without a difficult climb, you hardly ever get a good view.

Summary

1. Find a quiet place.
2. Get comfortable.
3. Unwind your mind.
4. Relax your body.
5. Relax totally for a while.
6. Move back – in a different gear.

I have suffered a great many calamities ... most of them never happened.

Mark Twain